✳ what's your IQ?

essentials

ken russell
& philip carter

foulsham
LONDON • NEW YORK • TORONTO • SYDNEY

foulsham

The Publishing House, Bennetts Close, Cippenham, Slough, Berkshire, SL1 5AP, England

We are indebted to our wives, both named Barbara, for checking and typing the manuscript, and for their encouragement in our various projects.

ISBN 0-572-02797-4

Originally published as *Check Your IQ*

Printed in Great Britain by Cox & Wyman, Reading

Contents

Introduction

About the Authors

Ken Russell and Philip Carter are continually devising new IQ tests and puzzles. During the past decade they have produced numerous books covering all aspects of testing and reasoning, including crosswords, word games, brainteasers and quizzes. Ken Russell is puzzle editor of *Mensa*, the general magazine of British Mensa, and Philip Carter is puzzle editor of *Enigmasig*, the newsletter of the British Mensa Special Interest puzzle group.

What is IQ?

IQ is the abbreviation for Intelligence Quotient. The dictionary definition of quotient is 'the number of times one quantity is contained in another'. The definition of intelligence is 'intellectual skill', 'mental brightness', 'quickness of mind'.

When measuring the IQ of a child, the child would attempt an intelligence test which had been given to thousands of children, and the results correlated so that the average score had been assessed for each age group. Thus, a child who at eight years of age obtained a result expected of a ten-year-old, would score an IQ of 125 by the following simple calculation:

$$\frac{\text{Mental age}}{\text{Chronological age}} \times 100 = IQ$$

$$\therefore \frac{10}{8} \times 100 = IQ$$

This does not apply to adults, whose assessment would be based on results correlated to known percentages of the population.

A child with a high IQ would have a great advantage at school with his or her studies, as understanding of lessons would be easily absorbed, but, in itself, a high IQ is not a key to success in later life. More important would be the qualities of competitiveness, personality, ambition, determination and temperament. In most walks of life, however, problem-solving is encountered and a person with a high IQ is well adapted to be successful in this field.

The average IQ is, obviously, 100. The population can be split roughly into three groups: 50 per cent would be between 90 and 110, 25 per cent would be above 110 and 25 per cent would be below 90.

Until recently, intelligence tests have been mainly related to knowledge of words, but with the advent of the increasing larger proportion of immigrants to Britain, whose knowledge of English could not perhaps be expected to be of a standard comparable to that of a native speaker, there is a swing towards culture-free tests. These are tests that use logic rather than word knowledge, so that diagrams are used instead of words. This makes no difference to the outcome, as spatial understanding and logical reasoning are good guides to one's degree of intelligence. These tests have also been standardised.

The eight tests which have been specially compiled for this book have not been standardised, so an IQ assessment has not been given. They are intended for practice for readers intending to take IQ tests in the future, and a guide is given as a check of success in undertaking each of these eight separate tests. There is also an accumulated score for performance in all eight tests.

It is now considered that one's IQ factor has a hereditary basis, but that it is possible to improve slightly by practice with IQ tests, but only marginally. Generally speaking, the IQ factor remains constant throughout life, tailing off slightly with age.

How to Use this Book

This book consists of eight separate tests, each of 50 questions. The tests are of approximately the same degree of difficulty. It is suggested that you tackle each test separately and note your score, after checking your answers against those given at the end of each test. A scoring chart for each test is also shown, one mark being awarded for each correct answer.

Each further test taken should show a slight improvement in your score, as practice will improve performance.

The total can then be taken for the eight tests and checked against the total scoring chart, shown below and also at the end of the book.

Each test has a time limit of 120 minutes which must not be exceeded.

Note: The answers to some of the questions have been explained. You may find these explanations useful if you are 'stuck' on certain types of question. In questions where you are required to find a missing word, the number of dots shown is equal to the number of letters in the word that you are looking for.

Total Scoring Chart for the Eight Tests

160–199	Average
200–239	Good
240–319	Very good
320–359	Excellent
360–400	Exceptional

Test 1

1   Which of the tiles A to H will fit logically into the space?

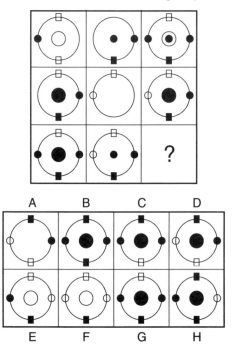

2

Which option below continues the sequence above?

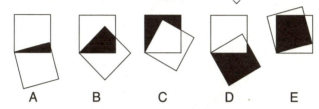

A   B   C   D   E

3 Which is the odd one out?

    bitch, hound, puppy, tabby, mongrel

4 Epistle is to letter as epithet is to:

    quip, name, speech, incident, archetype

5 Underline the two words which are closest in meaning.

    low, flush, ruffle, level, develop, sane

6 Which word inside the brackets is always part of the word outside the brackets?

    DERRICK (bowsprit, oar, vent, boom, anchor)

7 Place two three-letter 'bits' together to equal hog cured as bacon.

sco, fli, tia, por, tor, tch

8 Underline the name given to a group of owls.

murmuration, parliament, rafter, pace, wisp

9 If femur is to leg, then carpus is to which of these?

wrist, shoulder, arm, foot, pelvis

10 Here are five sets of faces.

Which pair below completes the set?

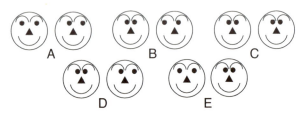

11 Underline which of these five words goes together with clip, weight and cup.

dance, strand, charm, chase, break

12 How many minutes before 12 noon is it, if one hour ago it was three times as many minutes after 8 am?

13 Which of A, B, C, D or E is the odd one out?

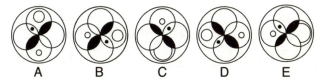

14 Which of these is the odd one out?

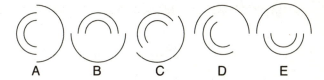

15 Insert a word that completes the first word and starts the second word.

win . . . . time

16   A B C D E F G H

Which letter is two to the left of the letter immediately to the right of the letter two to the right of the letter immediately to the right of the letter which is four letters to the left of the letter immediately to the right of the letter E?

17 Insert the missing number below.

9		19		18		14		10		16
	276				216				?	
7		14		6		9		14		7

18 Underline the two words which are opposite in meaning.

despondent, autocratic, optimistic, nostalgic, cautious, steadfast

19 Underline two words which mean the same.

travel, distrain, revolve, seize, vanish

20 Which word inside the brackets is never part of the word outside the brackets?

MAIGRE (vegetables, fish, tripe, eggs)

21 Which word means the opposite of bounteous?

hypothetical, niggardly, liberal, rewarding, grateful

22 Underline the odd name.

Hoover, Kennedy, Bolivar, Jefferson, Eisenhower

23 Find the missing number.

79,   87,   ? ,   89,   83

24

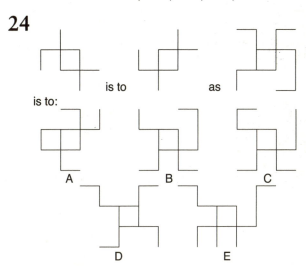

25 Which word inside the brackets is closest in meaning to the word in capital letters?

DETACH (specify, separate, withhold, uncover, reserve)

26

is to

as

is to

A

B

C

D

E

27 Which of these is the odd one out?

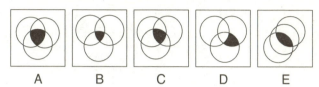

A   B   C   D   E

28 Here are six synonyms of the word 'fasten'.

chain, connect, secure, attach, bolt, grip

Take one letter from each word, in order, to spell out a further synonym of the word 'fasten'.

29 Abridge is to shorten as dilute is to:

decline, weaken, limit, relax, mitigate

30 Insert the word that means the same as the definitions outside the brackets.

originator (. . . . . . .) collapse and sink

31 Which of the following is not a vegetable?

HRCYCOI
CNSIAHP
LCCEARO
SPRIAPN

32 How many squares are there in this sketch?

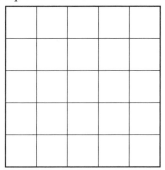

33 Underline the two words which are opposite to each other.

treelike, hyperborean, southern, windward, eerie

34 Solve the anagram (one word).

bare miles

35 Which word means the same as grampus?

dolphin, grandpa, intruder, school, cat

36 Which word continues this sequence?

square, pentagon, hexagon, septagon, ?

37

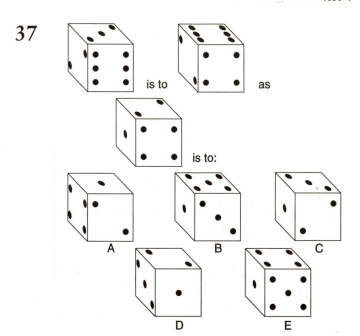

is to

as

is to:

A   B   C

D   E

38 Which of A, B, C, D or E is the odd one out?

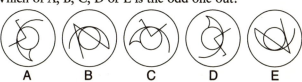

A   B   C   D   E

39

Which option below continues the sequence above?

A   B   C   D   E

40 Here are six antonyms of the word 'obliterate'.

construct, form, make, establish, generate, formulate

Take one letter from each word, in order to spell out a further antonym of the word 'obliterate'.

41 Which is the odd one out?

subscription, money, bonus, rebate, stipend

42 Which two letters complete this sequence?

ND, ND, ESD, NES, RS, ID, ?

43 What is the next number in this sequence?

1, 3, 8, 19, 42, 89, ?

44 Insert a word that completes the first word and starts the second word.

DRAW . . . . . . HEAD

45 Solve the anagram (one word):

Dresden

46 Which of squares A to H is the missing one?

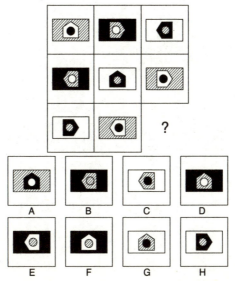

47 What is a mutchkin? Is it:

(a) a measure (b) a sprite (c) mutton
(d) a baby (e) a muscle?

48 Which of the tiles A to H will fit logically into the space?

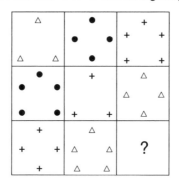

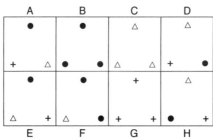

49 Insert a word that means the same as the words outside the brackets.

tree (. . . . .) aircraft

50 Which of the tiles A to H will fit logically into the space?

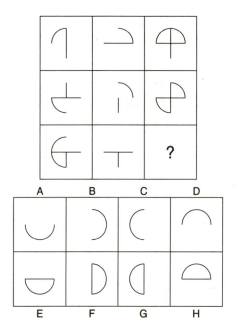

Answers to Test 1

1   G. (Column 2 is added to Column 1 to produce Column 3. Row 2 added to Row 1 produces Row 3.)

2   B. (There are two squares. One remains stationary. The second square gradually rotates. The shaded section moves from the top to the middle to the bottom area, in turn.)

3   tabby. (The rest are dogs.)

4   name

5   flush, level

6   boom

7   flitch

8   parliament

9   wrist

10 D. (There are four eye positions: left, right, centre and squint. D completes every possible pairing of the four eye positions.)

11 chase. (These four words can all have the prefix 'paper'.)

12 45 minutes

13 B. (A is the same as D, rotated, and C is the same as E, rotated.)

14 D. (The rest are identical but rotated to different positions.)

15 some

16 D

17 34.
$$((9+14) \times (19-7) = 276$$
$$(18+9) \times (14-6) = 216$$
$$(10+7) \times (16-14) = 34)$$

18 despondent, optimistic

19 distrain, seize

20 tripe

21 niggardly

22 Bolivar

23 81. (The differences are $+8$, -6, $+8$, -6.)

24 B. (The figures are flipped over vertically.)

25 separate

26 C. (They spell the words BENIGN and LASCAR.)

27 D. (In the others, the section common to all three circles is shaded.)

28 anchor

29 weaken

30 founder

31 LCCEARO.
(Anagram of CORACLE. This is a boat. The vegetables are chicory, spinach, parsnip.)

32 55

33 hyperborean, southern

34 miserable

35 dolphin

36 octagon

37 E. (The die rolls over one turn.)

38 C. (A is the same as D, rotated, and B is the same as E, rotated.)

39 C. (The circle which starts on the right is moving over the circle which starts on the left, half a diameter at a time.)

40 create

41 money

42 UR. (The middle letters from the days of the week.)

43 184. (Each of the numbers is doubled and 1, 2, 3, 4, 5, 6 is added in turn, so $89 \times 2 + 6 = 184$.)

44 bridge

45 reddens

46 D. (Each horizontal and vertical line of squares contains a black, a white and a striped section. The arrows point left, right and up in each line of squares.)

47 (a)

48 B

49 plane

50 C. (Column 1 is added to Column 2 to produce Column 3, but where lines or curves in Columns 1 and 2 coincide, they are deleted in Column 3. Similarly for the rows.)

Scoring Chart for Test 1

20–24 Average
25–29 Good
30–39 Very good
40–44 Excellent
45–50 Exceptional

Test 2

1 Which of the tiles A to H will fit logically into the space?

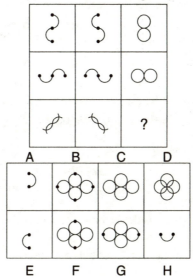

2 Which word inside the brackets is opposite in meaning to the word in capital letters?

REAR (starboard, stern, bow, yard, poop)

3

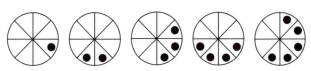

Which option below continues the sequence above?

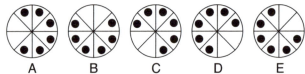

   A   B   C   D   E

4   Which word below goes together with age, rule and rod?

rabbit, club, ball, eagle, albatross

5   What creature is missing from the brackets?

hole (fox) trot

feed (. . . . . . .) out

6   Which word inside the brackets is always part of the word outside the brackets?

GARGOYLE (arms, spout, hat, spectacles, pince-nez)

7   Place the two three-letter 'bits' together to equal a two-masted vessel.

fal, iot, lug, gal, len, ien

8 If parapet is to roof, then fumarole is to which of these?

chimney, volcano, skylight, mountain, iceberg

9 Underline the name that is given to a group of hermits.

assembly, bench, caste, fraternity, observance

10 Which word below goes together with case, worm and mark?

coat, slide, pitch, station, jacket

11 Which of the shapes A to E is the odd one out?

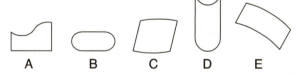

A   B   C   D   E

12 Fill in the missing number.

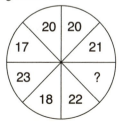

13 On glancing through your morning newspaper, you notice that four pages are missing. One of the missing pages is page 10. The back page of the newspaper is page 32. What are the numbers of the other three missing pages?

14 Underline the two words which are closest in meaning.

total, equate, compose, speak, compare, itemise

15 Which word inside the brackets is never part of the word outside the brackets?

MERINGUE (currants, egg, sugar, cream)

16 Which word below means the opposite of gaucherie?

awkwardness, ugliness, suaveness, brilliance, insistence

17 Underline the odd word out.

stalls, circle, scenario, fauteuil, box

18 Underline the two words which mean the same.

cursive, obstructive, flowing, repulsive, static

19 Find the missing number in the sequence.

31, 28, ? , 30, 31

20

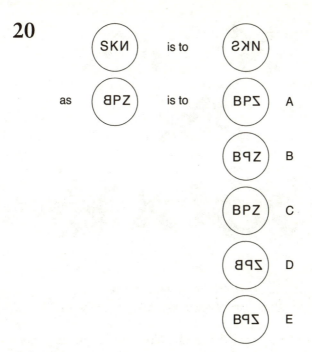

SKИ   is to   ƧKN

as   ꓭPƧ   is to

ꓭPƧ   A

ƧPꟻ   B

BPZ   C

Ƨꟼꟼ   D

ꓭꟼƧ   E

21 Which of A, B, C, D or E is the odd one out?

A   B   C   D   E

22

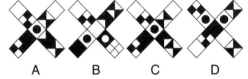

is to

as

is to

A   B   C   D

23 Graphic is to descriptive as rapture is to:

alacrity, ecstasy, burst, composure, voracity

24 Insert the word that means the same as the definitions outside the brackets.

noisy quarrel (. . . .) become ragged

25 Which is the odd one out?

calligraphy, artistry, chirography, writing, scribble

26

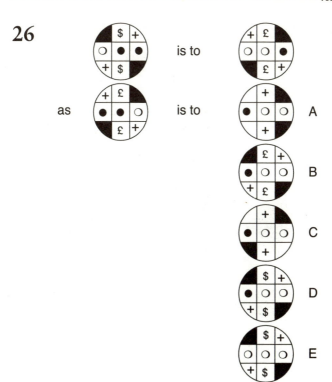

is to

as

is to

A

B

C

D

E

27 Which word continues the sequence?

cesspool, damp-course, transome, eaves

Choose from: reredos, moulding, loft, doorstep

28 What are the next two numbers in this sequence?

2, 1, 4, 3, 6, 6, 8, 10, ?, ?

29

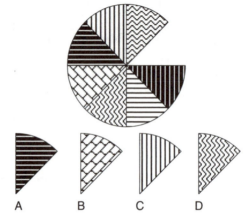

A   B   C   D

Which of the segments, A, B, C or D is missing from the above circle?

30 Solve the anagram (one word).

rivet wine

31 Fill in the missing word.

SEEN (LIKENESS) SILK

QUIT (. . . . .) YALE

32

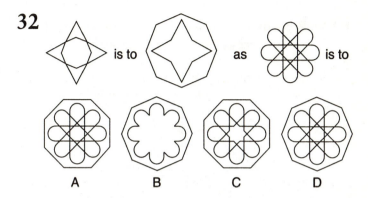

A B C D

33 Quixotic is to romantic as visionary is to:

idealistic, realistic, peace, reforming, belief

34 Insert the same number three times into this equation as it stands, to make it correct.

$$5 + 12 = 13$$

35 Which of A, B, C, D or E is the odd one out?

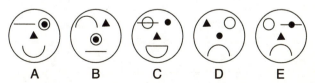

A B C D E

36 Underline the two words which are opposite to each other.

tapes, fauces, lips, taps, lupus

37 Which of the tiles A to H will fit logically into the space?

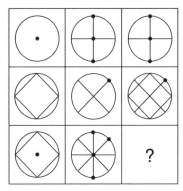

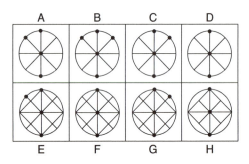

38 Here are eight synonyms of the word 'bogus'.

false, phoney, dummy, forged, artificial, counterfeit, fraudulent, sham

Take one letter from each word, in order, to spell out a further synonym of the word 'bogus'.

39 Which is the odd one out?

joke, laugh, chortle, titter, snigger

40 Which word means the same as the two words outside the brackets?

conceal (. . . .) skin

41 Solve the anagram (one word).

some great

42 Place the word in the brackets that means the same as the words outside the brackets.

alone (. . . .) fish

43 What is a tiro? Is it:

(a) a jewel   (b) a bird   (c) a peasant
(d) a novice   (e) a flume?

44 Insert a word that completes the first word and starts the second word.

chain . . . . bag

45

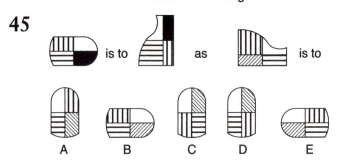

is to ... as ... is to

A   B   C   D   E

46 Which one of the following is not one of the seven virtues?

THRYIAC CPEUNRED OGNTUYTL TAFIH DFERUITOT

47 DEED, NOON, OCEAN, SEED, ?

Which word below continues the sequence above?

REAP, CAST, FLY, AUDIT, MINIM

48 Which of A, B, C, D or E is the odd one out?

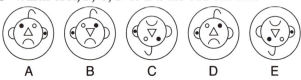

A   B   C   D   E

49 Which word means the same as scarab?

beetle, weapon, ruffian, ghost, dervish

50 Which of the tiles A to H will fit logically into the missing space?

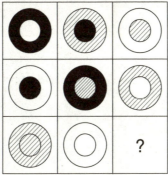

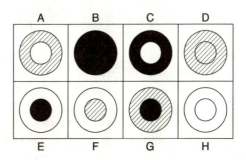

Answers to Test 2

1 D. (Rows and columns are added and black dots deleted.)

2 bow

3 B

4 eagle. (All four words can be prefixed by 'golden'.)

5 chicken

6 spout

7 galiot

8 volcano

9 observance

10 jacket. (All four words can have the prefix 'book'.)

11 A. (The only figure which has no symmetry, and also it has three straight lines, only one curved line and a double curve.)

12 19. (Start at one '20' and, in a clockwise direction, jump alternate sectors adding one. Start at the other '20' and, in a clockwise direction, jump alternate sectors deducting one.)

13 pages 9, 23 and 24

14 equate, compare

15 currants

16 suaveness

17 scenario

18 cursive, flowing

19 31. (The number of days in each of the first five months of a non Leap Year.)

20 E

21 B. (A is the same as D, and C is the same as E, when black and white are reversed.)

22 C. (One strip is put across the other to form a cross so that the middle segment is common to both. All black areas change to white and all white areas change to black.)

23 ecstasy

24 fray

25 artistry

26 D

27 loft

28 10, 15. (Two series: 2, 4, 6, 8, 10 and 1, 3, 6, 10, 15).

29 B. (In opposite segments, the lines of the patterns are the other way round.)

30 interview

31 EQUALITY. (Anagrams.)

32 C. (The middle pattern is removed and encases the original figure without the middle pattern.)

33 reforming

34 $5^2 + 12^2 = 13^2$

35 D. (It does not contain a line. All other figures contain a line, a circle, a dot, a triangle and an arc.)

36 fauces, lips

37 G

38 spurious

39 joke

40 hide

41 gasometer

42 sole

43 (d)

44 mail

45 A. (The original figure is turned on its end and changes to the second shape.)

46 GLUTTONY. (The virtues are charity, prudence, faith and fortitude.)

47 AUDIT. (The first two letters of each word are the same as for the months December, November, October, September.)

48 B. (A and C are the same, with C upside down, D and E are the same, with E upside down.)

49 beetle

50 B

Scoring Chart for Test 2

20–24 Average
25–29 Good
30–39 Very good
40–44 Excellent
45–50 Exceptional

Test 3

1 Which of the tiles A to H will fit logically into the space?

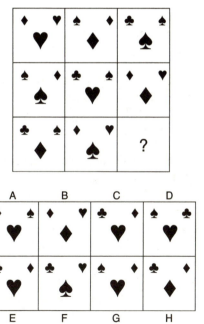

2 Which of A, B, C, D or E is the odd one out?

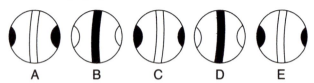

A   B   C   D   E

3 Insert the three missing words.

MANE		NAME

RATE	TARE	

	PALE	PLEA

4 Which word inside the brackets is opposite in meaning to the word in capital letters?

JAUNTY (wary, quiet, rough, staid, hostile)

5 Underline the name given to a group of princes.

pride, tiding, state, assembly, budget

6 Place two three-letter 'bits' together to equal the armpit.

lla, bes, axi, pue, oms, bro

7 Which of the squares A to H is the missing one?

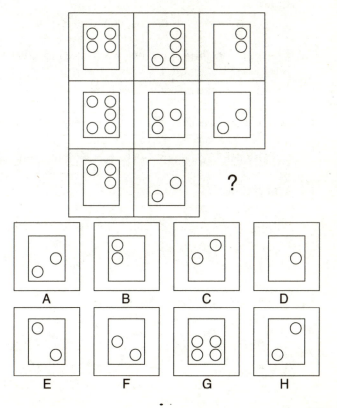

8 If canal boat is to gondola, then privateer is to which of these?

coracle, junk, corsair, schooner, corvette

9 Underline which of these five words goes together with jack, board and guard.

magic, judge, switch, den, party

10 Which word inside the brackets is always part of the word outside the brackets?

LORGNETTE (legs, wheels, rudder, motor, handle)

11 Which of A, B, C, D or E is the odd one out?

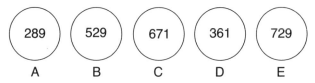

289	529	671	361	729
A	B	C	D	E

12 Which of A to E is the odd one out?

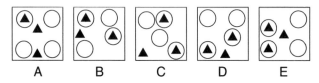

A   B   C   D   E

13 How many minutes past 11 am is it, if two hours ago it was three times as many minutes past 8am?

14 Underline the two words which are closest in meaning.

infernal, malicious, rude, demonic, parasitic, deranged

15 Which is the odd one out?

Dwight, Woodrow, Zachary, Cleveland, Ulysses

16 Which word means the same as the two words outside the brackets?

noise (. . . . .) intact

17 Which word inside the brackets is never involved with, or part of, the word outside the brackets?

EPAULETTE (wrist, shoulder, badge, officer)

18 Underline the odd word.

centime, moidore, brocket, piastre, pistole

19 Underline the two words which mean the same.

pendulous, finery, finesse, artifice, artifact

20 Find the missing number.

2, 12, 1112, ? , 132112, 1113122112

21 Which word means the opposite of austral?

occidental, southern, northern, mountainous, hilly

22

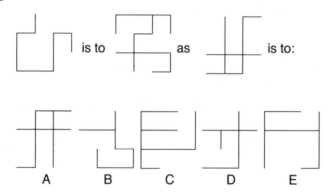

A   B   C   D   E

23 Here are five antonyms of the word 'domesticated'.

ferocious, savage, unbroken, untamed, wild

Take one letter from each word, in order, to spell out a
further antonym of the word 'domesticated'.

24 Read clockwise to find a word in each circle. You have to provide the missing letters. The two words are synonyms.

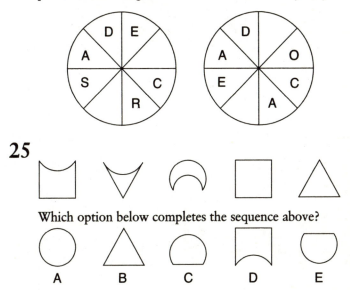

25

Which option below completes the sequence above?

A   B   C   D   E

26 Hilt is to sword as helve is to:

handle, whip, axe, knife, cup

27 Which of the tiles A to H will fit logically into the missing space?

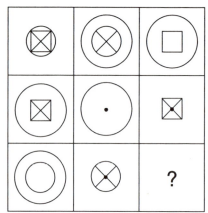

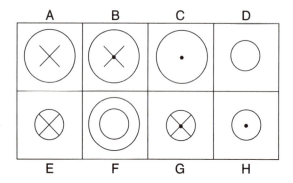

28 Insert the word that means the same as the definitions outside the brackets.

crude dwelling (. . . . . .) kind of song

29 Which word means the same as jocose?

sad, plump, merry, plausible, capable

30 Underline the two words below which are opposite to each other.

sallow, shallow, fallow, cultivated, hollow

31 What is the name given to a group of foxes? Is it:

(a) a smuck (b) a stand (c) a sloth
(d) a skulk (e) a spring?

32 Which word continues this sequence?

Duke, Marquess, Earl, Viscount

Choose from:

Count, Prince, Squire, Baron, Lord

33 Solve the anagram (one word).

liver base

34

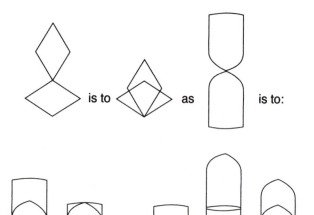

A   B   C   D   E

35   A B C D E F G H
Which letter is two to the right of the letter immediately
to the left of the letter three to the right of the letter
immediately to the left of the letter E?

36 Fill in the missing word.

ARCH (ENCROACH) CONE
GRIN (. . . . .) FINE

37

 is to

as is to:

 A

 B

 C

 D

 E

38 Which of the options A, B or C, when fitted to the piece shown here, will form a perfect square?

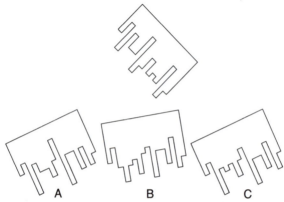

39 Fill in the missing number.

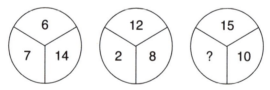

40 Place a word in the brackets that means the same as the words outside the brackets.

cloud (. . . . . .) halo

41 What is Shinto? Is it:

(a) a card game (b) a guard
(c) a religion (d) a dress (e) a scarf?

42 Solve the anagram (one word).

brief rake

43 Insert a word that completes the first word and starts the second word.

news . . . . . chase

44 Which of A, B, C, D or E is the odd one out?

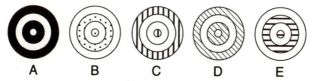

A   B   C   D   E

45 Which word inside the brackets is opposite in meaning to the word in capital letters?

PRUDENT (sagacious, open, permissive, extensive, improvident)

46 Which is the odd one out?

plait, tie, interlace, braid, intertwine

47 Dilemma is to quandary as plight is to:

danger, predicament, puzzle, confound, bewilderment

48 Which is the odd one out?

TFHORUERE

OTNWEO

SNEIVNEEN

FSIIVXE

49 Which of A, B, C, D or E is the odd one out?

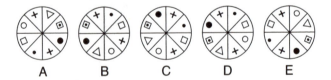

A   B   C   D   E

50 Which of the tiles A to H will fit logically into the space?

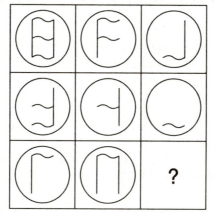

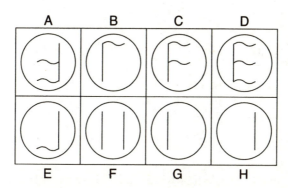

Answers to Test 3

1   G. (Each column and row contains: a large heart, diamond and spade; a small diamond, spade and club in the left corner; a small heart, diamond and spade in the right corner.)

2   E. (A is a mirror image of C and B is a mirror image of D.)

3   MEAN, TEAR, LEAP. (The three words in each line are anagrams in alphabetical order.)

4   staid

5   state

6   axilla

7   D. (Looking across and down, only circles common to both the first and second squares are carried forward to the third square.)

8   corsair

9   magic. (These four words can all have the prefix 'black'.)

10 handle

11 C. (The rest are square numbers:
$17^2 = 17 \times 17 = 289$ $23^2 = 23 \times 23 = 529$
$19^2 = 19 \times 19 = 361$ $27^2 = 27 \times 27 = 729$)

12 A. (In all the others there are two triangles in circles.)

13 30 minutes

14 infernal, demonic

15 Cleveland. (It is the surname of an American president and the others are first names.)

16 sound

17 wrist

18 brocket

19 finesse, artifice

20 3112. (Each number describes, when spoken, the previous number.)

21 northern

22 E. (One put on top of the other forms a complete square grid.)

23 feral

24 CRUSADER, ADVOCATE

25 E. (Each figure turns over and the curved line straightens. The resulting figure then moves three places to the right in the sequence.)

26 axe

27 B. (Add Column 1 to Column 2, similar symbols disappear, place answer in Column 3. Similarly for the rows.)

28 shanty

29 merry

30 fallow, cultivated

31 (d)

32 Baron

33 revisable

34 B. (The top figure falls to the bottom of the bottom figure.)

35 H

36 INFRINGE. (Anagrams.)

37 A. (Follow the same pattern in changing Xs and Os.)

38 C

39 2. $(15 \times 2 \div 3 = 10)$

40 nimbus

41 (c)

42 firebreak

43 paper

44 C. (In the others, alternate segments are shaded.)

45 improvident

46 tie

47 predicament

48 SNEIVNEEN. (In the others, the first, third, fifth etc letters, and then the second, fourth, sixth, etc spell out numbers that are consecutive.)

49 B. (A is the same as D, rotated; C is the same as E, rotated.)

50 H. (Column 1 and Column 2 add to produce Column 3, but where lines or curves in Column 1 and 2 coincide, they are deleted in Column 3. Similarly for the rows.)

Scoring Chart for Test 3

20–24 Average
25–29 Good
30–39 Very good
40–44 Excellent
45–50 Exceptional

Test 4

1   Which of the tiles A to H will fit logically into the space?

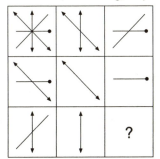

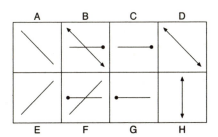

2   Grace is to Archbishop as Venerable is to:
     Countess, Cardinal, Canon, Archdeacon, Bishop

3 If flatfish is to plaice, then bivalve is to which of these?

sea-horse, octopus, trout, oyster, squid

4 Underline which of these five words goes together with cup, finger and brick.

sand, dog, paper, wind, nugget

5 Which word inside the brackets is always part of the word outside the brackets?

TOURNEDOS (beef, cream, lamb, cheese, pork)

6

Which option continues the above sequence?

A   B   C   D   E

7 Which word inside the brackets is opposite in meaning to the word in capital letters?

PALE (attractive, happy, fair, bilious, florid)

8 Underline the two words which are closest in meaning.

valuable, sterling, distinct, shiny, new, genuine

9 Here are seven synonyms of the word 'decrease'.

diminish, reduce, abate, shrink, curtail, dwindle, lessen

Take one letter from each word, in order, to spell out a further synonym of the word 'decrease'.

10 Which of the five boxes, A, B, C, D or E, is most like the box on the left?

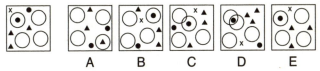

A   B   C   D   E

11 What is the missing number?

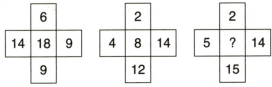

12 Which word inside the brackets is never part of the word outside the brackets?

QUADRILLE (cards, dance, four, playground)

13

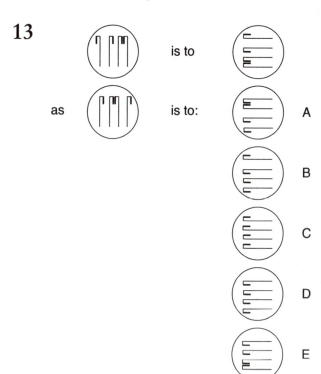

is to

as

is to:

A

B

C

D

E

14 Which word means the opposite of opulence?

sourness, poverty, riches, shiny, dull

15 Read clockwise to find a word in each circle. You have to provide the missing letters. The two words are synonyms.

 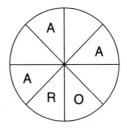

16 Underline the odd word.

trapezium, octagon, ellipse, circle, cylinder

17 Underline the two words which mean the same.

hidden, canine, biscuit, doggo, cylinder

18 Find the missing number.

37, 41, ? , 47, 51

19 Which word inside the brackets is closest in meaning to the word in capital letters?

PARAGON (fortress, section, pattern, leader, statement)

20

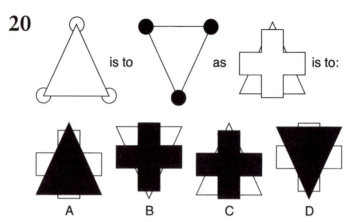

21 Insert a word that completes the first word and starts the second word.

do . . . less

22 Underline the two words which are opposite in meaning.

trip, rive, strive, join, place

23 Which word continues the list?

Pat, Terry, Jackie, Hillary,

Choose from:

Regina, Melanie, Bobby, Imogen

24 Which is the odd one out?

cyan, carmine, cobalt, azure, cerulean

25 Which of the tiles A to H will fit logically into the space?

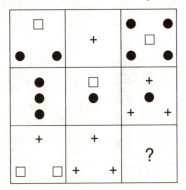

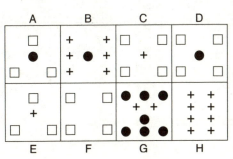

26 Place a word inside the brackets that means the same as the words outside the brackets.

recline (. . . .) slender

27 Which of squares A to D is the missing one?

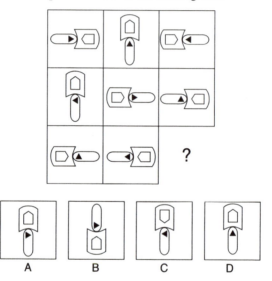

A   B   C   D

28 Solve the anagram (one word).

I sell a pub

29 Which number should be placed at '?'?

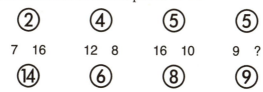

30 Which of the shapes A to E is the odd one out?

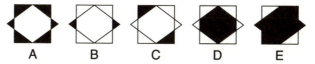

31 Which word means the same as chough?

dry, rough, puff, crow, chewy

32 Fill in the missing number.

33 Which is the odd one out?

encyclopedia, novel, dictionary, lexicon, thesaurus

34 Sierra is to mountains as savannah is to:

desert, valley, swamp, grassland, forest

35 Which of A, B, C, D or E is the odd one out?

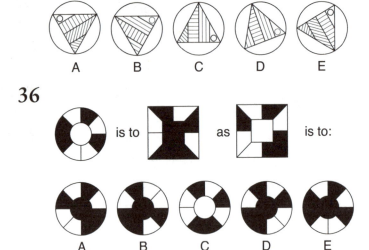

A   B   C   D   E

36

A   B   C   D   E

37 Insert the word that means the same as the definitions outside the brackets.

contrive (. . . . .) engrave or draw lines

38 Which of the following is not a bird?

> NGOPIE
> GEAMIP
> LOOIRE
> NTAUEP
> OFCNLA

39 Solve the anagram (one word).

> tribal ace

40 Insert a word that completes the first word and starts the second word.

> false . . . . wink

41 What is a kraal? Is it:

> (a) a game (b) a canal (c) a snake
> (d) a village (e) a woodpecker?

42 Insert a word that means the same as the words outside the brackets.

> grating (. . . . .) cook

43 Underline the name that is given to a group of squirrels.

> dray, erst, rush, convocation, dopping

44

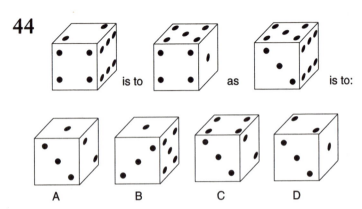

A   B   C   D

45 Fill in the missing number.

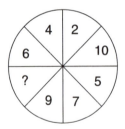

46 Underline the two words which are opposite in meaning.
worried, livid, confused, lifeless, delighted, irritable

47 Which of the tiles A to H will fit logically into the space?

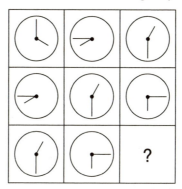

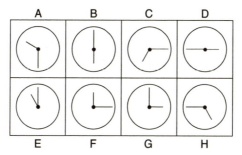

48 Place two three-letter 'bits' together to equal Russian whips.

uls, uts, pro, kno, cks, tro

49

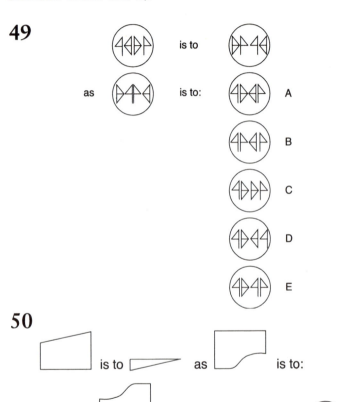

50

Answers to Test 4

1 E

2 Archdeacon

3 oyster

4 nugget. (These four words can all have the prefix 'gold'.)

5 beef

6 C

7 florid

8 sterling, genuine

9 subside

10 B. (It contains four circles [none of which intersect], three
   triangles, two dots including one in a circle] and one
   cross.)

11 10. ($2 \times 15 \div 3 = 10$ and $5 \times 14 \div 7 = 10$)

12 playground

13 A. (All hooks reversed.)

14 poverty

15 PROSPECT, PANORAMA

16 cylinder

17 doggo, hidden

18 43. (Consecutive prime numbers.)

19 pattern

20 D. (The drawing is turned over. The figure at the back comes to the front and is black instead of white.)

21 use

22 rive, join

23 Bobby. (Unisex names.)

24 carmine

25 C. (Making each dot = 1, each cross = 2 and each small square = 3, Column 1 is added to Column 2 to equal Column 3. Similarly for rows.)

26 lean

27 A. (So that each horizontal and vertical line of squares has each component pointing right, left and upwards.)

28 plausible

29 20. (When numbers outside the circles are multiplied together and divided by the numbers inside the circles, the answer is 4, i.e., $(9 \times 20) \div (5 \times 9) = 4$.)

30 B. (A and D, C and E have reversed black and white.)

31 crow

32 4. (Start at 10 and, moving round clockwise, jump alternate sectors, deducting one, then two, then three, then four.)

33 novel

34 grassland

35 C. (A is the same as E, rotated, and B is the same as D, rotated.)

36 D. (Squares become circles, circles become squares, and black and white are reversed.)

37 hatch

38 NTAUEPO. (Anagram of peanut. The birds are pigeon, magpie, oriole, falcon.)

39 calibrate

40 hood

41 village

42 grill

43 dray

44 D. (The die is turned over twice.)

45 1. (Opposite sectors total 11.)

46 livid, delighted

47 E. (Each clock advances 4¾ hours left to right and top to bottom.)

48 knouts

49 A. (Each shape in the circle rotates, vertically, through 180°. If there is a lower diagonal line, this is removed; if there is no lower diagonal line, one is added.)

50 A. (The figures added together form a rectangle.)

Scoring Chart for Test 4

20–24	Average
25–29	Good
30–39	Very good
40–44	Excellent
45–50	Exceptional

Test 5

1 Which of the tiles A to H will fit logically into the space?

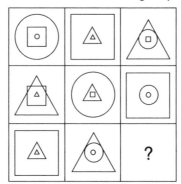

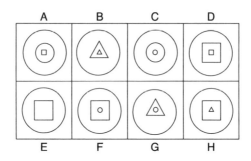

A   B   C   D

E   F   G   H

2 To which of the five boxes A, B, C, D or E can a dot be added so that both dots meet the same conditions as in the box on the left?

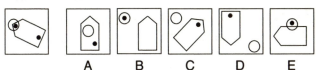

A   B   C   D   E

3 Read clockwise to find a word in each circle. You have to provide the missing letters. The two words are synonyms.

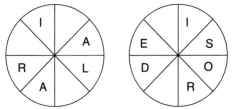

4 Here are eight antonyms of the word 'minor'.

considerable, profound, important, great, serious, vital, major, appreciable

Take one letter from each word, in order, to spell out a further antonym of the word 'minor'.

5 Underline the odd word.

hackney, felucca, droshky, flivver, trolley

6 Find the missing number.

169, 225, ? , 361, 441

7 Which word means the opposite of dulcet?

sweet, discordant, beautiful, shiny, musical

8 Underline the name given to a group of knaves.

deceit, pitying, rayful, desert, exhibition

9 Which of these is the odd one out?

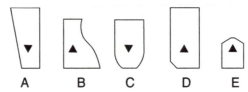

A   B   C   D   E

10 Fill in the missing number.

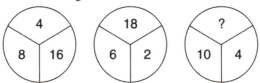

11 Flourish is to thrive as contrive is to:

succeed, scheme, prevail, accede, replace

12 Which word can be inserted in both sets of brackets to form other words with the addition of the letters on either side of the brackets?

S (. . .) H
C (. . .) H

13

(634) is to (97)

as (543) is to:

(87) A

(79) B

(78) C

(98) D

(97) E

14

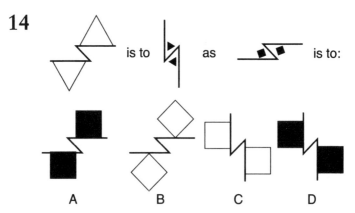

A   B   C   D

15 Underline the two words which are opposite in meaning.

urge, agree, enjoy, attack, secure, abhor

16 Insert the word that means the same as the definitions outside the brackets.

rod (. . .) unit of pressure

17 Solve the anagram (one word):

heed larks

18 If flora is to floral, then fauna is to which of these?

vegetable, fish, animal, bird, seed

19 Which word inside the brackets is always part of the word outside the brackets?

GUACAMOLE (avocado, pineapple, rum, brandy, peppers)

20 Underline which of these five words goes with plane, sickness and side.

duster, sugar, rifle, man, top

21 Which letter continues this sequence?

T, L, H, Z, M, ?

Choose from: E, F, K, N, V

22 Which of A, B, C, D or E is the odd one out?

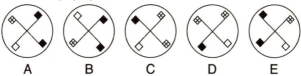

A B C D E

23 Apprehend is to understand as ascertain is to:

glean, learn, determine, memorise, remember

24 Which is the odd one out?

pentagon, pentathlon, pentode, penthouse, pentameter

25 Which of squares A to H is the missing one?

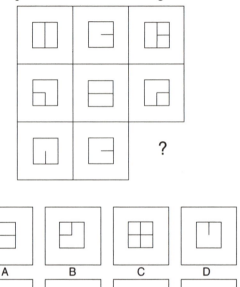

26 Vivace is to brisk as legato is to:

short, fast, slow, smooth, loud

27 Which of A, B, C, D or E is the odd one out?

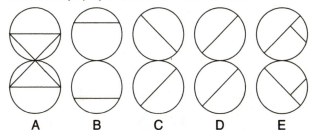

A   **B**   **C**   **D**   **E**

28 Underline the two words which are closest in meaning.

stagnate, complain, maunder, pester, thrash, meander

29 Which word inside the brackets is never part of the word outside the brackets?

VULCANISE (rubber, harden, sulphur, iron)

30 What is a parashot? Is it:

(a) a drug (b) a parasite (c) a parakeet

(d) a shot-putter (e) a marksman to shoot paratroops?

31 Insert a word that means the same as the words outside the brackets.

horse (. . . .) chop

32 Which word means the same as welkin?

drain, wrinkle, sky, storm, bells

33 Solve the anagram (one word).

dead liver

34

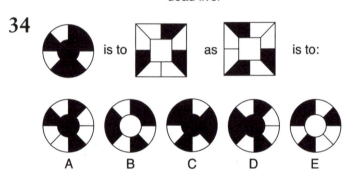

35 What is the decimal value of $\frac{5}{8} + \frac{7}{12} - \frac{5}{6}$?

36 Which word inside the brackets is closest in meaning to the word in capital letters?

PALATE (tongue, regal, taste, surface, board)

37 Which word means the same as the two words outside the brackets?

affirm (. . . . .) territory

38 Which of the tiles A to H will fit logically into the space?

MT	LI	N
IV	T	I
F	I	?

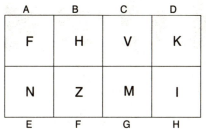

A	B	C	D
F	H	V	K
N	Z	M	I
E	F	G	H

39 Which of A, B, C, D or E is the odd one out?

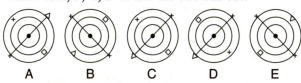

A   B   C   D   E

40 Which box of the five boxes A, B, C, D or E is least like the box on the left?

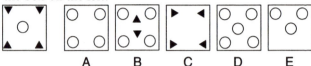

A   B   C   D   E

41 Fill in the missing number.

42 Which of the following is not a vehicle?

ROTESOC
IHTROCA
RAOTTCR
BNSMUIO
PCLEALS

43 Place two three-letter 'bits' to equal excessive fondness.

age, ade, ice, dot, pom, sol

44 Underline the two words which are opposite to each other.

doctor, mufti, Mohammedan, uniform, sword

45 Which word is part of this group?

mainsail, foresail, gaffsail, stormsail

Choose from: mistral, plimsoll, spinnaker, flotsam

46 Underline the two words which mean the same.

report, felon, artist, artisan, workman

47 Insert a word that completes the first word and starts the second word.

partner . . . . wright

48 What are the next three circles in this sequence? Choose from A, B, C, D or E.

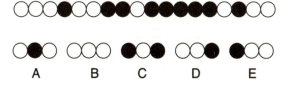

A   B   C   D   E

49   A B C D E F G H

Which letter is two to the left of the letter immediately to the left of the letter which is four to the right of the letter immediately to the left of the letter which is two to the left of the letter D?

50 Which of the tiles A to H will fit logically into the space?

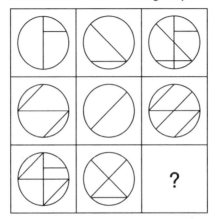

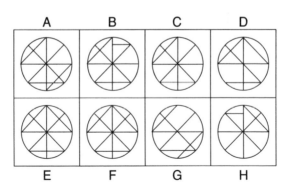

Answers to Test 5

1   D. (Completes the set. The sequence now contains three
    large, medium and small circles, squares and triangles.)

2   A. (So that when the dot is added it is in both shapes and
    the circle contains one dot only.)

3   farcical, derisory

4   superior

5   felucca

6   289. (The sequence is 13^2, 15^2, 17^2, 19^2, 21^2.)

7   discordant

8   rayful

9   D. (In the others, the arrow points to the narrowest side.)

10 25. (The square root of $25 \times 4 = 10$.)

11 scheme

12 LOT

13 E. (The first and second digits are added, and the second and third digits are added.)

14 C. (The diagram turns upright, the small black squares change to large white squares.)

15 enjoy, abhor

16 bar

17 sheldrake

18 animal

19 avocado

20 man. (These four words can have the prefix sea.)

21 E. (The first two letters of the sequence are each made up of two lines, the second two of three lines, the third two of four lines.)

22 A. (B and E are the same but rotated; C and D are the same but rotated.)

23 determine

24 penthouse. (The prefix pent does not mean 'five'.)

25 F. (Looking across, any lines common in the first two squares disappear in the third square. Looking down, only lines common to the first two squares are carried forward to the third square.)

26 smooth

27 D. (In all the others, the top circle is a mirror image of the bottom circle.)

28 maunder, meander

29 iron

30 (e)

31 hack

32 sky

33 daredevil

34 C. (The first figure is flipped over vertically. Black changes to white and white to black; circles become squares and squares become circles.)

35 0.375

36 taste

37 state

38 C. (Each letter in the boxes is made up of straight lines. Each straight line scores 1 point. Column 2 is taken away from Column 1 to give Column 3, and similarly for the rows. Thus,
6 – 3 = 3; 3 – 2 = 1; 3 – 1 = 2)

39 C. (A is the same as D, rotated, B is the same as E, rotated.)

40 E. (It has an incomplete pattern. The others have both lateral and vertical symmetry.)

41 16. (0 + 2 = 2, 2 + 2 = 4, 2 + 4 = 6, 4 + 6 = 10, 6 + 10 = 16.)

42 PCLEALS. (Anagram of scalpel. The vehicles are scooter, chariot, tractor and omnibus.)

43 dotage

44 mufti, uniform

45 spinnaker

46 artisan, workman

47 ship

48 B. (Splitting the circles into groups of three, the circles turn black one at a time from left to right and then white, one at a time, from right to left.)

49 B

50 G. (Rows and columns added together.)

Scoring Chart for Test 5

20–24 Average
25–29 Good
30–39 Very good
40–44 Excellent
45–50 Exceptional

Test 6

1 Select the missing tile from the six alternatives.

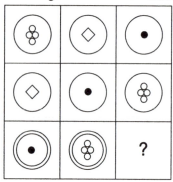

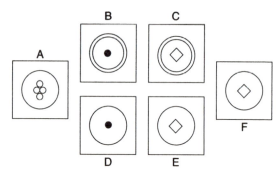

2 Which of these is the odd one out?

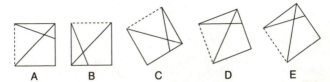

A   B   C   D   E

3 Underline the two words which are opposite in meaning.
prosaic, matchless, sentimental, mediocre, divergent,
tangled

4 some, rail, made
Which word below goes with the three words above?
man, shake, fine, treat, train

5 Underline the two words which are closest in meaning.
Ruritania, Eden, Acheron, Atlantis, Utopia, Cockaigne

6 Which word means the opposite of egress?
egret, departure, exit, tigress, entrance

7 Underline the name that is given to a group of ravens.
kindle, gaggle, fraternity, unkindness, mute

8 Find the missing number.

21, 34, ?, 89, 144

9 Underline the odd word.

lemming, racoon, limner, caribou, bubalis

10 Which of these is the odd one out?

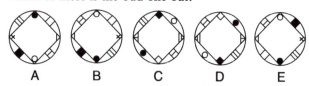

A   B   C   D   E

11

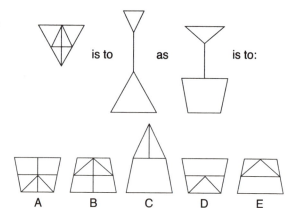

A   B   C   D   E

12 Which of squares A to H is the missing one?

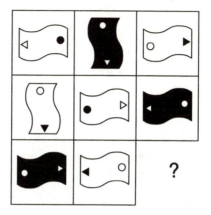

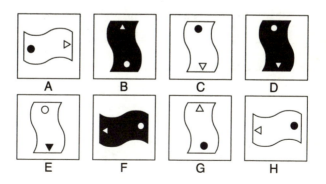

13 Fill in the missing number.

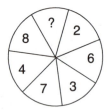

14 Here are six synonyms of the word 'gentle'.

peaceful, bland, compassionate, merciful, benign, tender

Take one letter from each word, in order, to spell out a further synonym of the word 'gentle'.

15 What is the next number in this sequence?

23, 48, 84, 133, ?

16 Solve the anagram (one word).

cur as fuel

17 Underline which of these five words goes together with ache, ward and gammon.

door, pane, meat, target, struck

18 If scalene is to triangle, then trapezium is to which of these?

quadrilateral, circle, oval, hexagon, pentagon

19 Which word inside the brackets is always part of the word outside the brackets?

TRIGONOMETRY (solids, calculus, progressions, algebra, angles)

20 Which of these is the odd one out?

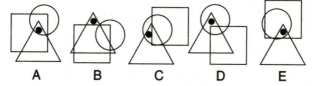

A   B   C   D   E

21 Which of the following is not a composer?

HMASRB
PHONIC
LMRHEA
ONERRI
GWREAN

22 Underline the two words which are closest in meaning.

lethargic, vituperative, sombre, virile, defamatory, corrupt

23 Which is the odd one out?

invalid, bedridden, void, inoperative, worthless

24

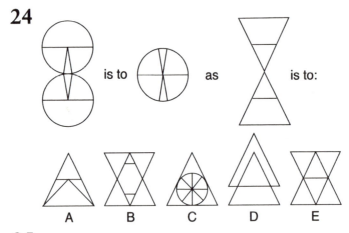

25 Fill in the missing word.

DREW (FOREWORD) ROOF

LOGO (. . . . .) PURE

26

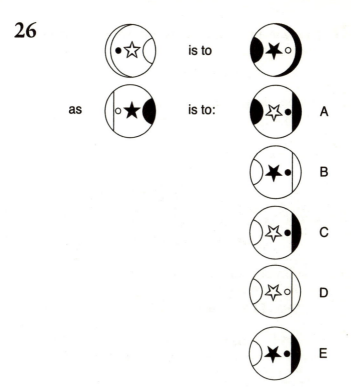

is to

as   is to:

A

B

C

D

E

27 Which word means a handle, a laughing stock, a bump and a barrel?

28 Place a word in the brackets that means the same as the words outside the brackets.

dog (. . . . . . .) soldier

29 Solve the anagram (one word).

bite metal

30 What is a fulmar? Is it:

(a) a fruit (b) a flag (c) a petrel
(d) a volcano (e) a penguin?

31 Which word means the same as mandrill?

weapon, fish, tool, baboon, bird

32 Which word inside the brackets is never part of the word outside the brackets?

SHILLELAGH (oak, cudgel, blackthorn, mulberry)

33 To which of the five boxes A, B, C, D or E can a dot be added so that it meets the same conditions as in the box on the left?

A   B   C   D   E

34 What is the missing number?

	5	
2	10	3
	4	

	9	
11	36	7
	8	

	7	
9	?	5
	8	

35 Below are eight antonyms of the word 'invincible'.

defenceless, weak, assailable, beatable, yielding,
vulnerable, conquerable, powerless

Take one letter from each word, in order, to spell out a
further antonym of the word 'invincible'.

36

Which option below continues the sequence above?

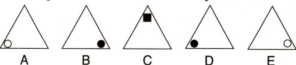

| A | B | C | D | E |

37 What number completes this sequence?

863937, 27216, 168, 48, 32, ?

38

 is to

as is to:

 A

 B

C

 D

 E

39 Insert the word that means the same as the definitions outside the brackets.

distribute (. . . .) plank of wood

40 Tenterhooks is to suspense as enamoured is to:
labour, love, DIY, memory, confidence

41 Which word is part of this group?
squash, lacrosse, tennis, baseball
Choose from: yoga, canasta, pelota, pugilism

42 Insert a word that completes the first word and starts the second word.

fort . . . . . mare

43 Underline the two words which are opposite to each other.
soft, valuable, paltry, spongy, stringy

44 Underline the two words that mean the same.
harmless, perfect, replete, innocuous, sane

45 Place two three-letter 'bits' together to equal a lewd fellow.
gol, rib, man, ase, ald, and

46 Insert a word that completes the first word and starts the second word.

AS . . . . OR

47

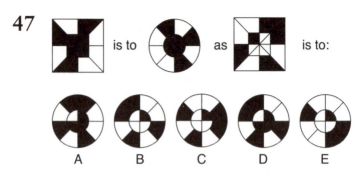

48   A B C D E F G H

Which letter is immediately to the right of the letter three to the left of the letter immediately to the right of the letter which is four to the right of the letter which comes midway between the letters A and C?

49 Which of these is the odd one out?

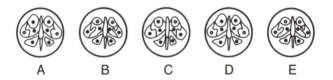

50 Select the missing tile from the six alternatives.

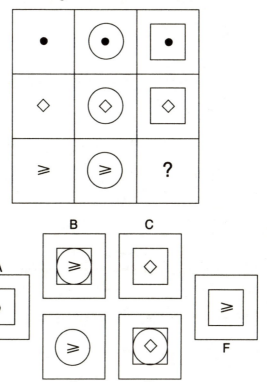

Answers to Test 6

1 C

2 B. (The others are rotations of the same figure.)

3 matchless, mediocre

4 shake. (These four words can all have the prefix 'hand'.)

5 Eden, Utopia

6 entrance

7 unkindness

8 55. (Fibonacci numbers – where each number is the sum of the two numbers preceding it.)

9 limner. (An illuminator of manuscripts.)

10 B. (A and E are the same, but rotated, and C and D are the same, but rotated.)

11 B. (The shapes at the ends of the vertical line are folded inwards.)

12 C

13 5. (Start at 2 and, moving round clockwise, jump alternate sectors, adding one each time.)

14 placid

15 197. (The differences are squares i.e. 5^2, 6^2, 7^2, 8^2.)

16 saucerful

17 door. (These four words can all have the prefix 'back'.)

18 quadrilateral

19 angles

20 B. (The only diagram in which the dot is not inside the circle; also the dot is in only one of the shapes.)

21 RENOIR. (The composers are Brahms, Chopin, Mahler and Wagner.)

22 vituperative, defamatory

23 bedridden

24 E. (The top part slides down over the bottom part.)

25 prologue. (Anagrams.)

26 C

27 butt

28 terrier

29 timetable

30 (c)

31 baboon

32 mulberry

33 D. (So that the dot appears in three circles.)

34 28. $(9 + 5 \times 2 = 28$ and $7 \times 8 \div 2 = 28.)$

35 fallible

36 D

37 6. (All the digits making up the previous number are multiplied together.)

38 E. (The letters in the circles are placed on top of one another.)

39 deal

40 love

41 pelota

42 night

43 paltry, valuable

44 harmless, innocuous

45 ribald

46 SAIL

47 B. (The figure is flipped over and changed into circles.)

48 E

49 C. (A and D are the same; B and E are the same.)

50 F

Scoring Chart for Test 6

20–24 Average
25–29 Good
30–39 Very good
40–44 Excellent
45–50 Exceptional

Test 7

1   Which of the tiles A to H will fit logically into the space?

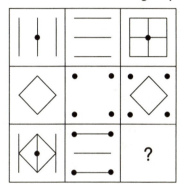

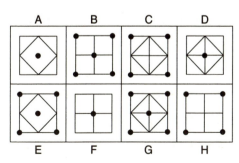

2

Which option below continues the sequence above?

A   B   C   D

3 What is the missing number?

4 Underline the two words which are opposite in meaning.
help, lead, subside, domineer, confute, intensify

5 Underline the name given to a group of hares.
plump, rie, muster, lepe, husk

6 Underline the odd word.
bustard, jackdaw, marabou, quetzal, lamprey

7 Find the missing number in this sequence.

10, 15, ? , 28, 36

8 Which word means the opposite of recalcitrant?

calculating, chalky, furious, submissive, rebellious

9

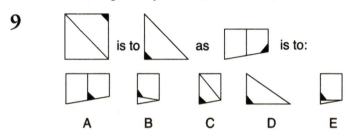

A   B   C   D   E

10 Which is the odd one out?

Mandingo, Masai, Maya, Zulu, Bantu

11   VACATE, PALATE, NEGATE, SIMILE, RELATE

Which word below would you choose to put with the words above?

ABROAD, NOVICE, STAMEN, LINEAR, SANITY

12 Insert the word that means the same as the two words outside the brackets.

pursuit (. . . .) breed

13 Which of the tiles A to H will fit logically into the space?

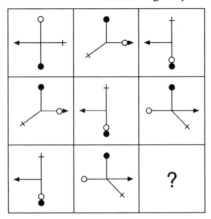

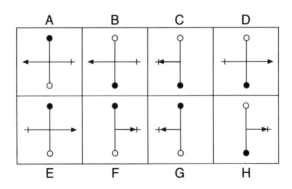

14

Which option below continues the sequence above?

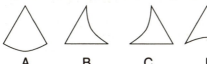

A   B   C   D   E

15 Which number continues this sequence?

130, 215, 300, 345, ?

16 Here are six synonyms of the word 'frail'.

brittle, feeble, vulnerable, decrepit, weak, breakable

Take one letter from each word, in order, to spell out a further synonym of the word 'frail'.

17 Which word inside the brackets is closest in meaning to the word in capital letters?

OSTRACISE (flaunt, appal, banish, beleaguer, chastise)

18 Underline which of these five words goes together with struck, chart and gazer.

worm, stage, wars, dance, law

19

One man can dig a trench in 2 hours
A second man can dig a trench in 3 hours
A third man can dig a trench in 5 hours
A fourth man can dig a trench in 6 hours

How many hours will it take to dig a trench if they all work together at their own speeds?

0.43, 0.63, 0.83, 1.03, 1.23

20 If Balaclava is to hat, then burnous is to which of these?

scarf, tie, hood, belt, shoe

21 Which word inside the brackets is always part of the word outside the brackets?

ZAPATEADO (whispering, sliding, clicking, swimming, climbing)

22 Solve the anagram (one word).

nose crane

23 Which of the following is not a tree?

APPLRO
IWWOLL
RECYHR
OLIVET

24 To which of the five boxes A, B, C, D or E can a dot be added so that both dots meet the same conditions as in the box on the left?

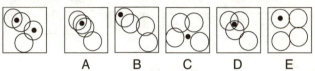

A   B   C   D   E

25 Insert the missing number.

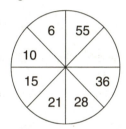

26 Which of A, B, C, D or E is the odd one out?

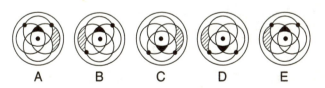

A   B   C   D   E

27 Which of A, B, C, D or E is the odd one out?

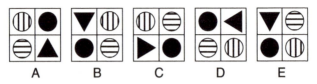

A   B   C   D   E

28 Insert the missing number.

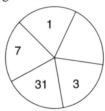

29 Fill in the missing word.

DIVE (DERISIVE) RISE

CORN (. . . . .) SAID

30 Which word inside the brackets is never part of the word outside the brackets?

MAUD (shepherd, woollen, plaid, Welsh)

31 Which word means the same as gelid?

pink, soft, cold, warm, jelly

32 Solve the anagram (one word).

reamer tap

33 Place a word in the brackets which means the same as the words outside the brackets.

balk (. . .) shy

34 What is a lazar? Is it:

(a) an Egyptian (b) a beam (c) a leper
(d) a churchman (e) a bazaar?

35

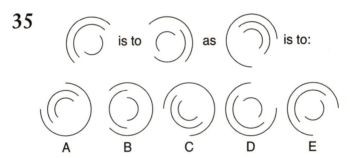

36 Place two three-letter 'bits' together to equal a narrow opening.

kni, cra, pru, che, nny, vat

37 Which of squares A to H is the missing one?

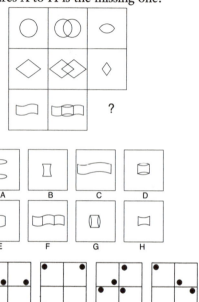

38

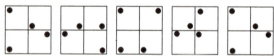

Which option below continues the sequence above?

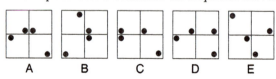

39

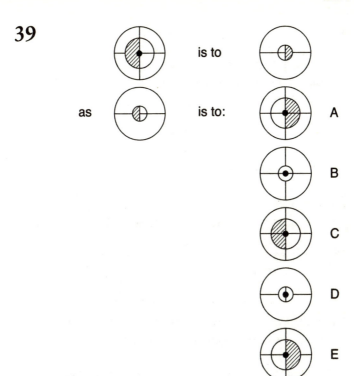

40 Which word means a small island, a solution and an operating lever?

41   A B C D E F G H

Which letter is four to the right of the letter immediately to the left of the letter immediately to the left of the letter which is three to the right of the letter immediately to the left of the letter B?

42 Which word is part of this group?

emerald, garnet, topaz, opal

Choose from: terrine, marcasite, porringer, tureen

43 Underline the words which are opposite to each other.

ghostly, wiry, frangible, unbreakable, paramount

44 Insert a word that completes the first word and starts the second word.

nut . . . . jack

45 Underline the two words which mean the same.

principal, fortnight, quotidian, daily, prefect

46 Which word inside the brackets is closest in meaning to the word in capital letters?

GRATUITY (payment, reward, freedom, appreciation, present)

47 Which word means the same as the two words outside the brackets?

embed (. . .) group

48

 is to

as is to:

 A

 B

 C

 D

 E

49 Nurture is to deprive as intrepid is to:
doughty, flinching, homely, charitable, submissive

50 Which of the tiles A to H will fit logically into the space?

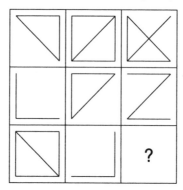

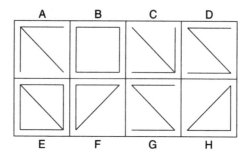

Answers to Test 7

1   G

2   D. (There are four triangles, each with its base on one side of the square. The height of the triangle increases by a quarter of the square side length each time.)

3   15. (19 – 4 and 17 – 2.)

4   subside, intensify

5   husk

6   lamprey. (A fish; the others are birds.)

7   21. (Triangular numbers.
$$4 + 3 + 2 + 1 = 10$$
$$5 + 4 + 3 + 2 + 1 = 15$$
$$6 + 5 + 4 + 3 + 2 + 1 = 21 \text{ etc.})$$

8   submissive

9   B. (The right side is folded back on to the left.)

10 Maya. (The others are African tribes.)

11 NOVICE. (The words have consonant and vowel alternately.)

12 race

13 C. (Vertically and horizontally; the arms with the small black circle and the arrowhead both advance 180° each time; the arm with the small white circle advances 90° and that with the cross bar advances 135°, each time.)

14 D. (Each side of the triangle, in turn, is curved out and then, in turn, curved in.)

15 430. (i.e. 4.30. They are times, each advancing 45 minutes, shown without the 'dot'.)

16 tender

17 banish

18 wars. (All four words can have the prefix 'star'.)

19 0.83 hours. (Which is ⅚ hour or 50 minutes.)

20 hood

21 clicking

22 resonance

23 OLIVET. (Anagram of violet. The trees are poplar, willow and cherry.)

24 B. (So that one dot is in one circle only and one dot is in two circles only.)

25 45. (Start at 6 and, moving round anticlockwise, add 4, then 5, then 6, etc.)

26 B. (A and D, C and E, are the same, but rotated.)

27 B. (The others are the same figure rotated.)

28 15. (Start at 1 and moving round clockwise, jump alternate sections, doubling and adding 1.)

29 SARDONIC. (Anagrams.)

30 Welsh

31 cold

32 parameter

33 jib

34 (c)

35 C. (The longer curve moves 90° clockwise. The two smaller curves move through 180°.)

36 cranny

37 B. (The middle segment of the central column is taken out, turned around and put into the right column.)

38 D. (The dot in each small square follows its own sequence.)

39 E

40 key

41 F

42 marcasite

43 frangible, unbreakable

44 cracker

45 quotidian, daily

46 reward

47 set

48 E. (The shapes in the circles represent the numbers 3, 2, 9 and 8, backed by their reflections.)

49 flinching

50 A. (Column 1 is added to Column 2 and lines common to both are deleted to make Column 3. Similarly for the rows.)

Scoring Chart for Test 7

20–24 Average
25–29 Good
30–39 Very good
40–44 Excellent
45–50 Exceptional

Test 8

1 Which of A, B, C, D or E is the odd one out?

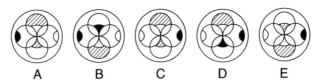

2 Which of the boxes A, B, C, D or E has least in common with the box on the left?

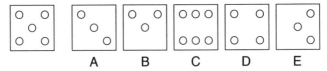

3 180 is to (9, 15, 20) as 84 is to:

(2, 6, 12), (3, 4, 12), (3, 4, 7), (6, 12, 8), (6, 7, 21)

4 Here are seven synonyms of the word 'rectify'.

correct, repair, amend, improve, reform, square, adjust

Take one letter from each word, in order, to spell out a further synonym of the word 'rectify'.

5 Which word means the same as the two words outside the brackets?

intend (. . . .) miserly

6 Which word means the opposite of quiescence?

querying, disagreement, repose, activity, agreement

7 Underline the name given to a group of horses at stud.

brood, grist, flight, harras, business

8 Find the missing number in this sequence.

192, 221, ? , 285, 320

9 Underline the word which is the odd one out.

pinnace, phaeton, currach, pontoon, gondola

10

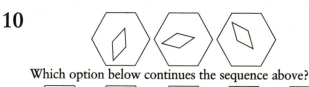

Which option below continues the sequence above?

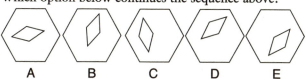

A   B   C   D   E

11 Which word inside the brackets is closest in meaning to the word in capital letters?

SYLLABUS (adolescent, vehicle, study, curriculum, idiot)

12 Which word is the odd one out?

tarn, mere, stream, loch, lake

13 Which of A, B, C, D or E is the odd one out?

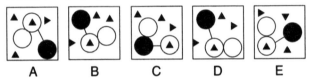

A   B   C   D   E

14 Read clockwise to find a word in each circle. You have to provide the missing letters. The two words are synonyms.

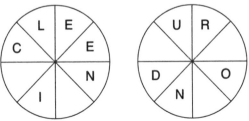

15 Which of the tiles A to H will fit logically into the space?

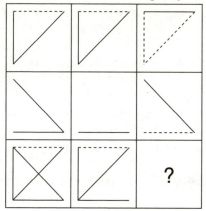

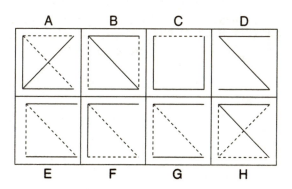

16 Underline the two words which are opposite in meaning.

clamorous, moderate, tiny, voracious, susceptible, sardonic

17 What is the next number in this sequence?

7, 27, 58, 102, ?

18 Which word inside the brackets is always a part of the word outside the brackets?

WORSTED (spots, wool, cotton, stripes, linen)

19 If Everest is to Himalayas, then Sierra Madre is to which of these?

Spain, Mexico, Brazil, Portugal, Chile

20 Solve the anagram (one word).

tune hopes

21 Underline which of these five words goes with stead, help and run.

corner, slide, time, hope, work

22

Which option below continues the sequence above?

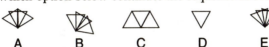

A   B   C   D   E

23 Insert the missing number.

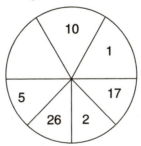

24 Insert the word that completes the first word and starts the second word.

prim . . . . bud

25 Which of the tiles A to H will fit logically into the space?

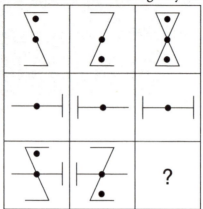

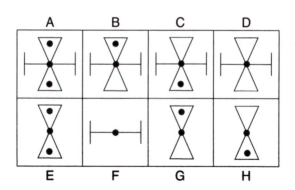

26 Which of these is the odd one out?

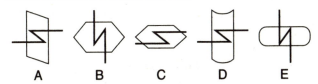

A   B   C   D   E

27 Which word means a tool, a drink and a blow?

28 Which word below goes with able, maker and time?

safe, ship, dive, tight, fully

29 Insert the same number twice into this equation as it stands, to make it correct.

16 × 2 = 8

30 Which word inside the brackets is never part of the word outside the brackets?

METHEGLIN (Welsh, liquor, honey, rum)

31 Solve the anagram (one word).

I rue ranch

32 Which word means the same as pensile?

horizontal, upright, hanging, prolonged, extensive

33 What is falcate? Is it:

(a) sickle-shaped (b) club-shaped
(c) pea-shaped (d) cross-shaped
(e) diamond-shaped?

34 Insert a word that means the same as the words outside the brackets.

bunting (. . . .) droop

35

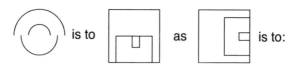

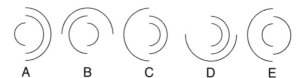

A B C D E

36

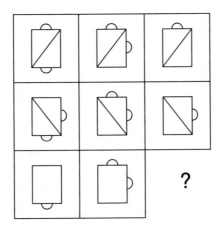

Which of squares A to H is the missing one?

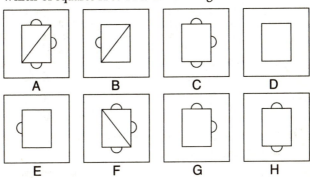

37

 is to

as is to:

 A

 B

 C

 D

 E

38 Insert the word that means the same as the definitions outside the brackets.

furnace (. . . . .) advance steadily

39 Connoisseur is to expert as vintner is to:

producer, merchant, wine, waiter, bottler

40 Underline the two words which mean the same.

invexed, depleted, diffident, pacify, concave

41 Which word continues this list?

Drake, Raleigh, Beatty, Nelson

Choose from: Brambell, Jellicoe, Hess, Garnett

42 Place two three-letter 'bits' together to equal a Spanish sheep.

ton, ino, lin, mer, cat, cot

43 Insert a word that completes the first word and starts the second word.

charge . . . . some

44 Underline the two words which are opposite to each other.

abundance, glory, dearth, revenge, bathos

45 Which of these is the odd one out?

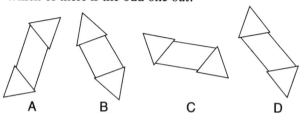

A   B   C   D

46   ONLY, TWIN, THAT, FOAM, FIST

Which word below continues the sequence above?

TSAR, SINK, TURF, MOVE, SELF

47 Which word can be inserted in all three sets of brackets to form another word with the addition of the letters on either side of the brackets?

L (. . .) R
M (. . .) Y
H (. . .) Y

48 How many minutes before 12 am is it, if one hour ago it was twice as many minutes after 9 am?

49

is to

as

is to:

 A

 B

 C

 D

 E

50 Which of the tiles A to H will fit logically into the space?

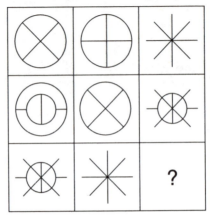

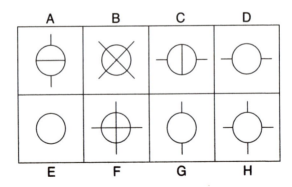

Answers to Test 8

1 C

2 C. (All the others are part of the figure on the left.)

3 (3, 4, 7). (84 is the smallest number into which these three numbers will divide.)

4 redress

5 mean

6 activity

7 harras

8 252. (This is $16^2 - 4$). The sequence is $(14^2 - 4)$, $(15^2 - 4)$, $(16^2 - 4)$, $(17^2 - 4)$, $(18^2 - 4)$.

9 phaeton

10 B. (The hexagon rolls over on to each base in turn.)

11 curriculum

12 stream. (The others are still water.)

13 C. (The empty circle is touching the black circle. In all the others it touches the other white circle.)

14 ENCIRCLE, SURROUND

15 H. (Column 1 is added to Column 2 to make Column 3. Where two dashed lines coincide, they become full lines; where two full lines coincide they become dashed. Similarly for rows.)

16 moderate, voracious

17 161. (The differences between the numbers are consecutive squares less 5. That is, the differences are: $5^2 - 5$, $6^2 - 5$, $7^2 - 5$, $8^2 - 5$.)

18 wool

19 Mexico

20 penthouse

21 work. (The four words can all have the prefix 'home'.)

22 C. (The bottom two triangles are swinging upwards an equal amount at a time.)

23 37. (Starting at 1 and moving clockwise, jump alternate sectors adding odd numbers, i.e. 1, 3, 5, 7, 9, 11.)

24 rose

25 A

26 C. (In all the others the 'lightning bolt' goes through the narrowest part of the figure.)

27 punch

28 fully. (The four words can all be prefixed with the word 'peace'.)

29 $16 \times 32 = 8^3$.

30 rum

31 hurricane

32 hanging

33 (a)

34 flag

35 C

36 D. (Horizontally and vertically, only lines common to the first two squares are carried forward to the third square.)

37 B

38 forge

39 merchant

40 concave, invexed

41 Jellicoe

42 merino

43 hand

44 abundance, dearth

45 B. (All the others are the same figure rotated.)

46 SINK. (The first two letters of each word are the first two letters of the numbers ONE, TWO, THREE, etc.)

47 ONE

48 40 minutes

49 C

50 A. (The first column is placed on top of the second column. Lines in common disappear and remaining lines are placed in the third column. Similarly for the rows.)

Scoring Chart for Test 8

20–24 Average
25–29 Good
30–39 Very good
40–44 Excellent
45–50 Exceptional

Total Scoring Chart for the Eight Tests

160–199	Average
200–239	Good
240–319	Very good
320–359	Excellent
360–400	Exceptional